Somewhere in the Cycle

Somewhere in the Cycle

Monica Flegg

Cover design: Shay Culligan
Cover photograph: Chloe Graves
Copy editor: Cindy Hochman of "100 Proof"
    Copyediting Services

ISBN: 978-1-949229-02-8

Kelsay Books
Aldrich Press
www.kelsaybooks.com

For my husband, Stuart Flegg,
for making the music of family life,
and believing in Nantucket's magic.

And to Blaise and Skye for expanding
my capacity for wonder.

Acknowledgments

Grateful thanks to the editors of the journals where these poems first appeared, sometimes in different form and/or with different titles.

"Rise" published in *Ancient Paths,* 2016
 "Galaxy in a Shark's Eye" published in *Eyedrum Periodically,* Fall 2017
"Somewhere in the Cycle" published in *the Aurorean,* Spring 2000
"Riptide" published in *Rat's Ass Review,* 2017
"Wonder" published in *Mothers Always Write,* 2016
"Sharing in the Stirring" published by *Nantucket Writings,* Summer 1999
"Summer Groove" published in *First Literary Review-East,* July/August 2018
 "Nest" published in *Dying Dahlia Review,* 2016
"Fluff with Fork" published in *Every Pigeon,* Issue 3, 2018

Islands are metaphors of the heart,
no matter what poet says otherwise.

—Jeanette Winterson, *Sexing the Cherry*

Contents

Some play as if they own
the world; others as if they
are receiving it.

The Machinery in Swans' Wings

The industrial creak of swans'
wings pulls my attention to the sky,
where they fly past, noisy as the
ferry winch, unceremonious
as an assembly line.

It surprises me that
these graceful waterfowl
lose their elegance
with loftiness and voice;
surely a matter to consider.

Galaxy in a Shark's Eye

My muse
   is a shifty sort
  wafting
in on a
steam of conscience
  fishtailing ideas to
    and fro
chiseling phrases from
  a coffin bone

   scenting them with
tropical lantana
      zigzagging curious
 and citrus
    like anyone could follow
  that crazy
rain
  of
thought.

 I want to add
   syllables
to
segue my sanity
 or
   run assistance to
 my imagined reader,
but

        I don't because
deep down
    I know
the fragments align
exactly
    like the
        galaxy
in a
  shark's eye.

Homing

The snowy owl and I
have site fidelity
Nantucket.

Rise

It's a winter of candy-apple cheeks,
crystal-cracked puddles,
and UGG-embossed snow stars.

The polar vortex makes possible
our backyard ice rink,
where blades of laughter cut

across frigid air
as my kids skate in the novelty
of their sky-roofed arena.

My son stops mid-glide,
slides his phone from his pocket
and texts me, "Cocoa please."

He could've waved and I would've
seen him from the kitchen window,
throne of motherhood, where I

watch my children whiz and spin,
hurtling forward, crashing down,
collapsing to their knees, then rising.

Nest

We squabble over the
temperature,
and Nest documents our
disagreement.

He moves it up
and I move
it
down.

This happened three
separate
times on November 30th
alone.

It's going to
be a long winter
nesting
together.

Morning Ritual

There's a bird's nest in my left hip; a
tangle of nerve endings gone haywire

threatening my forward progress toward
Mellon Field, where my Golden will pose

his paws handsomely on the picnic
bench and await his mini Milk-Bone.

No searing wire nest in my joint
will rob me of this simple joy;

watching my boy in the morning sun
in a field full of birdsong and snow.

The Most Wonderful Time of the Year

Glass ornaments and
children go together like
cake and horseradish.

Mothers hate glitter
in invitations and cards;
trust me on this one.

Dogs will roll in deer
carcasses just before your
guests arrive with wine.

The treetop will scar
the newly painted ceiling;
sap will be sticky.

So will peppermint
candy canes sugaring up
your careening elves.

You will want to day-drink
the day you decorate.
Trust me on this too.

I Had a Dream

My winter of discontent
might just as well be called
winter of *Deadliest Catch* reruns.

Oh, the unending nature of the storms
seaming us in with double stitching.
Those double-digit snow measurements
giving hemmed-in high definition.

The nightly news blaring weather alerts
seemed exciting through about
Martin Luther King Day.

After that I had a dream, and it
billboarded destinations like
Daytona Beach. I dreamt warm
sand and shimmering pavement.

I fantasized bare feet, but in reality
I wore my blasted snowshoes, which
are a nuisance to fasten even without

our Aussie yapping
around my ankles,
desperate for his daily walks.

Around February, Stuart and I
sank into a desensitized couch slouch.
We languidly approached everything; even
pressing the button on the remote

seemed like a strain. I'm pretty sure
I completed four years of college with
less effort than it took to click off
Flip This House.

Those Property Brothers were so close
but so far away—
just like spring.

Ready for Market, Indeed!

My dog and I put on a little
weight this winter and his
vet tech said, "He's ready for market,"

which I didn't think necessary,
even if it was a joke, but nevertheless
we're braving another Nor'easter

walking away from the weight that
was this winter; heading toward
lightness.

Boundless

My 6-foot-tall teenager moves like a panther,
powerful and elegant with sprite-light footfall.
Even when he's wearing steel-toed Timberlands and
hauling lumber lengths into organized stacks, there's
self-control stowed below his purposeful stride.

Watching his energy uncoil, springing into:
imagination; guinea pig-powered space ships,
invention; hybrid race and street bikes,
motion; leaping tabletops, flying across berm.
My heart leaps to the beat of his boundless potential.

The Knitters

Valentine mochas and Miles Davis
sweeten The Bean this
crystal-bright February night
while I wile away an hour
during my daughter's orchestra practice.
She's rehearsing for the Beethoven
Festival late this March,
when Islanders' ears will hear
multiple generations of musicians
playing the "Ode to Joy."

A clutch of women gathering to knit
settle around the corner tables,
softly talking stitching, cables,
and YouTube tutorials
as they fawn over silky alpaca fiber.
I glance at yesterday's paper,
bold headlines bland in
comparison to the knitters' thrum.

Clicking needles
as regular as breathing,
they layer a new rhythm over
the jazz and speakeasy
yarn of rich pleasures.
"Smoky pink peppercorns,
saffron skeins, micro-batches,
musk, lanolin, distilleries, bottles."
They weave words that
have a nose.

My appetite rises
for big bands, busy hands,
pomegranate poems, and
mocha valentines.

String Recital

After all the little children
play their
"Twinkle Twinkles"
and Suzuki standards,
Skye steps softly to
the front of the room and
plays her cello like a sunrise
and a heartbreak, a birth and
a death; the strings furiously
paddle upriver,
then recede, as the
audience
floats
downriver,
finishing
in a place of awe.

Somewhere in the Cycle

Spokes spin sails
and spirit me skyward.
I soar high above
bike paths and bane
in fanciful sphere
of the warbler's world.

Rising, rising,
watching spider's webs
wane to silken threads.
Poems penetrate
my hollow bird bones,
cawing blood
from every cloud.

Splashed on moors,
crimson plants
lie flat like
bright blankets
for picnickers
feasting on words.

I flash past
a jetting monarch,
am reminded midair
of tortoise and hare.
Caution, faithless,
flings me down,

until wheels
wobble on blacktop,
talons shift,
hands brake.

Watery Edges

People who live on islands
tend to like water borders,
which are really just
tidings and invitations.

Invasive Species

on Nantucket include:
chinaberry with
its indigo fruit;
English holly, icon
of holiday tradition;
and wild mustard
with its perfectly edible
leaves. Also Japanese
knotweed and bamboo, just
to name a few.

They come with their flaunts
and their flaws, just
like other island visitors;
tourists. We wish
they settled into our
island less loudly,
we wish they were
less ornamental, more
traditional,
or just plain edible.

Perspective

The only thing worse than a rainy day with a house full of guests on Nantucket is a house full of guests on a rainy day anywhere else. Also a bunch of other things are worse, but this is a prose poem and really shouldn't drag on.

Like a rainy day
on Nantucket with a house
overrun by guests.

Quiet as Quakers

A committee of
turkey vultures rests
in trees
quietly.

Quietly because
they have no
voiceboxes, rendering
them
squawkless,
cackleless.

P.S. Also harmless.
    They don't kill.

Has there
ever been a bird
with a more undeserved
PR problem?

They swoop down
to clean another's mess
by picking ceaselessly
at the carcass.

Once they're grounded,
picking bones,
they're called
a wake. And

I'd rather gather at a wake
with these humble outcasts
than those soaring, squawking
swans garnering praise.

Fishing

We choose lures
like charms
from a salty
gray bait box,
then tie lines,
flip bails,

c—
    a—
        s—
            t—

hoping for a bite
for a bass
for a bit.

Summer Groove

The others wear navy blazers as
comfortably as I wear a swimsuit,

talk at fundraising soirées as
smoothly as swans swim.

Their private jets deposit them
on Nantucket the second week

of August and the Island feels
heavy with their expectation, thick

as their helps' apprehension. They
try to look casual at the brewery

or on the beach. Haircuts
and unfaded swimsuits signal

their status. Other as their means
are, we're all sailing in the Sound,

swinging at Summer Groove; in
love with the same island.

Riptide

It was that summer of '88
the August that we tempted fate.
Treading naked in the Madaket rip,
swimming toward each other's grip.

Feeding desire until we ached
crawling beachward exhausted, faint.
Covered with sea moss, collapsing on shore,
resting for a while, then wanting more.

We hungered further along that course
physical indulgence with no remorse.
The gluttony of that insatiable season
knew no bounds, knew no reason.

Our skins waned from fevered prowl,
but our love fattened on that fowl.

For Skye

Being a second child is
like tubing behind a boat,
riding in its wake,
learning to maneuver
over it,
to smoother, unoccupied
waters, where there's
no limit to your imprint.

Wonder

Will adulthood heave our children
into an unrecognizable place
full of concrete, deadlines,
and obligations so
sizable that they stop
marveling at an inchworm's moves?

A place where mass transit
and technology
attempt to trump the
Cooper's hawk's dives and glides,
his purposeful vision
searching prey.

Will the roar of engines
making their way
across interstates
lull them to sleep
instead of the sound
of surf stroking sand?

Or will their childhood spent
crawling through deer paths
and huckleberry-scented moors
keep alive their
taste for color?

Sunny cinquefoil, violet vetch,
and wild strawberries
usher in spring before
they race into summer on
glimmering waves—their bodies
angling boards on foaming crests.

Our kids ride in
with red tide and bluefish,
covered with sand and salt;
their glowing skins
radiate like the future
on an altar of praise.

September

I watch Clorox pooling on the counter,
bleaching away coffee stains, bacon grease,
and gray grit from lottery card scrapings,
along with blisters of melted ice cream.

Five minutes later I strong-scrub the grout
with a firm white-and green-bristled brush. The
methodical movement of my wrist keeps
the bleach from splashing while I wash away

summer's decadence and slide into school-
year mode. Here come the nutritious meals, dry
bathing suits, apricot tea, and the clean
clarity of a silent childless house.

Fluff with Fork

Even instructions on Minute Rice
flummox me; am I
fluffing with fork correctly?

Am I making a good enough meal?
Am I a good mom? Good wife?
Good, good, good … it's as
monotonous as all those oo's.

Excellence has smoother sounds.
But no quinoa or organic
vegetables tonight—just
chicken, marginal onions, and a bruised
pepper—stir-fried into dinner

served with *fluffed with fork* rice
and grace, that amazing grace,
which turns good to excellent
every single time.

Sharing in the Stirring

When you near the stove to
oversee my steaming of the sugar snap
peas, it's like coming inside to warm
cocoa after shoveling snow on
a freezing morning,

like collapsing on a sun-soaked beach
towel after swimming in the June ocean,
like finding the missing piece,
finding it right beside me, sharing
in the stirring of summer vegetables.

Heart's Desire

If I write a book it
will have an orange
jacket.

If I have a dog he'll
have alert brown
eyes.

If I eat dessert it'll
be ice cream laden
with butterscotch.

If I have my heart's desire
it'll always be you, Stuart,
always you.

No Other Place

If made to leave my Island, my keening would
carry over the waves and echo off the jetties,
causing sun-drenched seals to lift their heavy heads,
their luminous eyes reflecting water like tears.

My heart would tug like a rip current, ache
like an empty womb, feel like a virtue
stripped from me. Without Nantucket, my own
identity would feel like a shadow on the sand.

My heart would still beat steadfast, like the
staccato call of the cormorant, but my
swooping joy would be stunted, like an osprey
gliding over marshes, unable to hunt.

Nourished by Nantucket for thirty years,
no other place is milk and honey for me.

Photograph by Laurie Richards

About the Author

Monica Flegg has lived on Nantucket Island since the day after she graduated from the University of Missouri School of Journalism. By then she had already figured out that there is more truth in poetry than in the newspaper. Nantucket has been her muse, her music, and her magic for thirty years. She lives there year-round with her husband and two children.

24483642R00026

Made in the USA
Columbia, SC
23 August 2018